↘↘↘↘
DEBRIDEMENT

BOOKS BY MICHAEL S. HARPER

DEBRIDEMENT
HISTORY AS APPLE TREE (1972)
HISTORY IS YOUR OWN HEARTBEAT
  (1971)
DEAR JOHN, DEAR COLTRANE (1970)

ᔰ ᔰ ᔰ ᔰ ᔰ ᔰ ᔰ ᔰ

DEBRIDEMENT

by Michael S. Harper

DOUBLEDAY & COMPANY, INC.

GARDEN CITY, NEW YORK 1973

"Corktown," "Caves," "Sitting at the Dais," "In the Projects," "Don't List," "A White Friend Flies in from the Coast," "Mama's Report," Circle of Bloods," "The Family of Debridement," first appeared in *Works in Progress*, No. 7; "Heartblow: Messages," in *New Letters*, Copyright © 1971 by the curators of the University of Missouri; parts of "History As Cap'n Brown" published in *Blacks on John Brown*, edited by Benjamin Quarles, University of Illinois Press.

ISBN: 0-385-00481-8

LIBRARY OF CONGRESS CATALOG CARD NUMBER 72-84918

COPYRIGHT © 1972, 1973 BY MICHAEL S. HARPER

PRINTED IN THE UNITED STATES OF AMERICA

FIRST EDITION

for ROLAND WARREN HARPER
PATRICE CUCHULAIN HARPER
RACHEL MARIA HARPER

the living

and for REUBEN MASAI
MICHAEL STEVEN

the dead,
torn away

ↆↆↆↆↆ

CONTENTS

PART II: HEARTBLOW

PART III: DEBRIDEMENT

WHEN THERE IS NO HISTORY
THERE IS NO METAPHOR;
A BLIND NATION IN STORM
MAULS ITS OWN HARBORS:
SPERMWHALE, INDIAN, BLACK,
BELTED IN THESE RUINS.

PART ONE

↘↘↘↘↘↘↘

HISTORY

AS

CAP'N

BROWN

HISTORY AS CAP'N BROWN

"MY NAME IS JOHN BROWN; I HAVE BEEN WELL KNOWN AS OLD JOHN BROWN OF KANSAS. TWO OF MY SONS WERE KILLED HERE TODAY, AND I'M DYING TOO. I CAME HERE TO LIBERATE SLAVES, AND WAS TO RECEIVE NO REWARD. I HAVE ACTED FROM A SENSE OF DUTY, AND AM CONTENT TO AWAIT MY FATE; BUT I THINK THE CROWD HAVE TREATED ME BADLY. I AM AN OLD MAN. YESTERDAY I COULD HAVE KILLED WHOM I CHOSE; BUT I HAD NO DESIRE TO KILL ANY PERSON, AND WOULD NOT HAVE KILLED A MAN HAD THEY NOT TRIED TO KILL ME AND MY MEN. I COULD HAVE SACKED AND BURNED THE TOWN, BUT DID NOT; I HAVE TREATED THE PERSONS WHOM I TOOK AS HOSTAGES KINDLY, AND I APPEAL TO THEM FOR THE TRUTH OF WHAT I SAY. IF I HAD SUCCEEDED IN RUNNING OFF SLAVES THIS TIME, I COULD HAVE RAISED TWENTY TIMES AS MANY MEN AS I HAVE NOW, FOR A SIMILAR EXPEDITION. BUT I HAVE FAILED."

THE PRICE OF REPRESSION IS GREATER THAN THE COST OF LIBERTY.

KANSAS AND AMERICA

Some hated slavery
Some hated blacks
Some hated slaves
All loved land

↗ ↗ ↗

THE MUSIC OF BROADSWORDS

We hacked them with broadswords:
our liquor dealer whose dive was the US court;
his brother-free-state-woman-baiter-bully;
our postmaster with no spit on his stamps;
our probate judge of warrants;
three slave-chasers who suckled their bloodhounds
in our muddy saloon: *Kansas*.

↗ ↗ ↗

"RESCUE WORK": DUES

Crowns from the south:
black gold in a red box
marked "spleened";
black bottom hands locked
to riverboats at the wrists;
a Mexican serape staked
to a cottonplant with bowie knife;
patrollers near Lawrence,
Swamp of the Swans:
long-necked birds
in an eagle snare,
their feet, paddling, in cotton.

↗ ↗ ↗

DREAMS: AMERICAN

At the rifle factory:
telegraph wires curl
in a one-horse wagon
taken where rivers
of blood wilt near
the armory gate—
60 rods more to the railroad
bridge towpath, making bullets—
my Lafayette sword,
wet powder, men
climbing into hillsides
of hostages we didn't kill;
screens of people we made
at the engine house we didn't use:
dead in the trestle work
in a moonless sky,
conspired in madness to steal

myself and steal away,
the mountaintop looks out,
its face the light
heartblow, a sword
upon the Golden Rule.

A scalp wound in a head rag
I pray out forty days
at the symbolic pallet:
put the insane in this pit,
dig to a subway pass:
the world is my family,
my brothers insane:
"insanity is like a very
pleasant dream to me."

↗↗↗

ALLEGHENY SHADOWS

The mountains call me
into arms of barricades,
its life-work
the economy-heart-
bloodbank in three phases:
black sloughs come after war
in English woolens;
black protection from duties,
cotton, ironworks, free trade;
black whirlwinds of gold

mushroom: industrial-
power-broker:
say we won't cooperate,
corner the market so we can circle
over our goods and bargain for ore.
Allegheny mountaintop:
an ensnared people on each fringe,
each settled, dollared ravine.

↗ ↗ ↗

PLANS

R ailroad routes;
Indian territory;
southern Missouri:

Douglass believed in Brown
but not in his plan:
a secret page of mountain
to strawbrick and turpentine.

These are accounts payable:
hidden arms in an Ohio haymow,
hung by the heavens in scarlet
on Blue Ridge Mountain,
even as the black phalanx fails;
though I am sick with ague,

truth fevers that new-made grave,
one thousand pikes as stones.

Earthwork inspections
from Roman provinces
to Spanish chieftains:
Schamyl, Circassian,
Moina, Toussaint, Hugh Forbes.

Hot bloody spots
at watered points—
Potomac/Shenandoah:
I pledge my life to each slave,
with iron rather than in iron.

↗ ↗ ↗

REPORTS: KANSAS

Osawatomie Brown
killed by pro-slavery
man named White—
Frederick Brown is dead—
Brown hit by spent grape
canister, rifle shot—
killed by scalping
so bruised he didn't know
it 'til he reached the place:
with irons in hand I take
my scalp as Dred Scott
is taken in irons:

Come to the crusade:
blood is the issue,
not Negroes, *brothers.*

ↆↆↆ

AMERICA CALLS!

Called out of Egypt,
mother and ewe lamb
dead, the woods sunken
red men speckled,
their tongues
chained to a tree,
songs of black oak
keyed to scrotum:
what to survey with my tools:
round limbs of woman,
six sons, one daughter,
fevered insanities
of woman and child, dead,
on the mountain is my path.

Tending our newborn,
I walk the uneven woodpile
singing to child,
wife, through the day,
my step charmed by light
of woodshed. I carry her
three nights 'til she died.
Both died in their cradled arms.

One marries a girl
five years older than my oldest
as fate and promise of death
grow like trees burning,
my family these leaves
edged on two new-made graves:
action, one life to live:
spirits of my first woman
make me *do*
under Allegheny sky.

Though England kills my wool
as I sell it,
farm, racehorse, tannery,
surveyor: 1837: embargoes kill:
war kills my woolens,
love surveyed Oberlin
for black schools.

I raised six hundred
Saxony lambs
for my English masters,
saw it sold to my American
neighbor-friend-middleman:
quality wool for cheap factories;
cheap religion gone business
beats the slave
with an iron shovel.

I was born May Day;
my father stuttered.
In September, 1800,
Gabriel was born;
my father stuttered.

Clear songs of the Indian,
a chained blackened piglet
roasts on its chain,
I stutter at my own color-caste.

↗↗↗

'EMPEROR': SHIELDS GREEN: FUGITIVES

Sunday Meeting: *I b'lieve I'll go wid de ole man.*
At Chambersburgh Quarry:
I guess I'll go wid de ole man.
Black Monday: *I must go down to de ole man.*

↗ ↗ ↗

GEN'L TUBMAN, AS WE CALL HER

$10,000: dead or alive won't catch her;
dreamer of dreams and sickness will:

"Serpent in rocks and bushes,
head of a white-bearded old man,
then two younger heads spoke:
Come!
I was sick,
dreaming wishful deeds:
the heads spoke in tongues."

While at writing table
two wrens flew in
from their porch nest
fluttering attention;
a snake on our post
set to eat our young in the nest;

father killed the snake,
the wrens' songs burst
a successful omen.

Heads as flowers
not birds,
and cut off
to blossom
on a table:
then I heard of Harper's Ferry.

↗ ↗ ↗

FOUR WORTHIES: SOULS OF BLACK FOLK

To *Know*, in heart, in groin;
to *Move*, trestle, bog, boat, mask;
to *Love*, woman, child, land, trees;
to *Aspire*, where blood, sperm, bone join.

↗ ↗ ↗

FUGITIVE PATHS

Submit, fight, run:
young woman
demented in childbirth,
a boy four dead:
Turner 'live and dead;
Crandall's burned school
checkers our stacked churches,
Lovejoy murdered,
Fayette's stories of woe:

I swear a blood-feud
with slavery,
my sword of Gideon
amidst this vast veil:
"it is right for slaves
to kill their masters and escape."
Plans form their towpaths
to arsenal gates,
Gabriel's glory, openended.

↗ ↗ ↗

SAMBO'S MISTAKES: *An Essay*

Weaknesses:
    small good reading,
    thrown money on luxury—
    no capital;
    servility,
    talkativeness,
    disunity,
    sectarian bias:
    expects security with whites
    by tamely submitting to
    indignity, contempt, wrong.

Strengths:
guns.

↗↗↗

"S.P.W.": JOURNEY OF CONSCIOUSNESS

These mountains are my plan:
natural forts conceal
armed squads of five
on a twenty-five mile line;
slaves run off
to keep them strong;
the infirm underground,
property insecure with blood:
"Subterranean Pass Way"

↗ ↗ ↗

"LEAGUE OF GILEADITES":
MESSAGES

Nothing so charms the American
people as personal bravery:
Cinques on *Amistad*,
Lovejoy and Torrey:
all traitors must die.
Count on division among whites:
teach them
not to throw fire
in a wooden house—
lasso slave-catchers:
hold on to your weapons:
man-stealing is *rescue work.*

↗ ↗ ↗

SOJOURNER TRUTH: BLACK SYBIL IN SALEM

Frederick, is God Dead?"

"No, and because God is not
dead, slavery can only end in blood."

↗ ↗ ↗

FORTY DAYS LOOKING
BACKWARDS: *Notes from a surveyor*

Negro Steven found Kansas
after Indians found the land in themselves;
Kansas found: 1820—
slave barons leap into Missouri,
rape Mexico, Kansas-Nebraska Bill.

Free Soilers hate slaves not slavery.
Harper's Ferry sieves the Great Black Way.
In Waverly
I buried a son in thunderstorm
dead of cholera,
was refused food by rebels:
ploughed: planted corn,
fruit trees, vines,
hay for the stock:
fever and ague and guns

came 'cross the borders
glutting the polls:
I sought funds for arms.

At Big Springs some hated
slavery, more Negroes,
many slaves; the Indians were gone:
Kansas slave, Nebraska free:
Brooks broke Sumner's head
in Senate chambers
for telling these facts:
border ruffians rode Missouri
lines blanketed with killing.

We made our own "constructive
treason" at "Dutch Henry" settlement
in the Swamp of the Swan:
death by broadswords.

I took my instruments
into their camp
"sound on the goose"
mistook-mapmaker for slavery:
Owen, Frederick, Salmon, Oliver:
chain carriers, axman, marker.
One Georgian said:
"them damned Browns over there,
we're going to whip, drive out,
or kill, any way to
get shut of them, by God"
while I made entries
in my surveyor's book
to strike the blow.
The Wakarusa "treaty" put
federal troops in slave power,
armed bands at "Dutch Henry";
when ruffians warned our women

must leave, they burned two houses, a store,
and we sharpened our cutlasses.

"I am aware that you hold
my two sons, John and Jason,
prisoners—" I wrote
on scraps of paper that saved their lives.
Five sons built earthworks
in a circle near Lawrence;
beans, johnny-cake, mush,
milk, pumpkin, squash:
Kansas white only.

While they made out warrants
we camped near Osawatomie
while I had my visions from God:
slaughter at Osawatomie.
With little free-state support
we set out corn bread, meat,
blankets, running bullets,
utensils, loading,
came together at Black Jack
surrounded by a chain of forts,
patrollers in cavalry uniform.

I looked at the symmetry of heaven,
rolled dry beef, corn bread
bruised between stones,
in the ashes, felt the nervous power
of Ezra's affliction:
reports from thick chaparral
had me dead; we captured the cannon
'Sacramento', joined Lane's
army at Nebraska City:
'No Quarter' was our motto.
The best battlement
is a well-armed guerrilla:
with an old wagon, cow,
a hidden slave, I slipped
through troops with surveyor tools,
disappearing from Kansas.

↗ ↗ ↗

JIM DANIELS: HAMILTON MASSACRE: *PARABLE*

From Fort Scott I met Jim Daniels
selling brooms as disguise,
handsome mulatto; less than a year
ago eleven citizens were gathered up
by armed force under Hamilton,
formed in a line without trial,
and shot: all left dead, all free-staters:

What action has the president,
governors of Missouri, Kansas taken?

Daniels came to Osage settlement
from Missouri, wife, children,
another black man to be sold next day,
asking for help: *rescue work* in Missouri.

Posse to "enforce the law":
man-stealing, no; killing free-staters,
yes: look up the barrel of this shotgun,
see if you can find your slaves.

↗ ↗ ↗

PLANS: 2

I proposed a Negro school in Hudson: 1828;
in 1858 I fixed Harper's Ferry as spring
to the Great Black Way, central depots
spurred the Alleghenies, mountain arsenal:
pikes, scythes, muskets, shotguns,
Sharpes rifles for skilled officers:
Forbes betrayed us in temper, money:
we delayed a year in fever.

At Chatham we met,
'League of Freedom':
swamped marooned,
Appalachian range,
Indian territory,
the rout of Gabriel.

Rifle ball words
on rifle ball tongue:
most who gave arms
wanted use in Kansas only;
blacks hid me in Springfield,
rumors of scalping in Hartford,
cache of Harper's Ferry
in a guerrilla handbook:
I am through with Plymouth Rocks,
Bunker Hills, Charter Oaks,
Uncle Tom's Cabins:
those held accountable
are the mighty fallen.

I am without horses, holsters,
wagons, tents, saddles, bridles,
spurs, camp utensils, blankets,
intrenching tools, knapsacks,
spades, shovels, mattocks, crowbars,
no ammunition, no money
for freight or travel:
I have left my family poorly:
I will give my life for a slave
with a gun my secret passage.

↗ ↗ ↗

'MANUEL FOR THE PATRIOTIC VOLUNTEER'

Enough talk about bleeding Kansas.
Douglass could not be convinced,
his children were more interested,
Kagi, Richardson, Stevens, Moffett,
Shields Green: dead letters:
black laws of black dead
from Cincinnati to Canada.

"Odd Fellows": De Grass, McCune Smith,
Purvis, Vashon, Woodson, the Langstons,
Gen'l Tubman, Henson, Douglass,
Loguen, Payne, Ogden, Ward,
Garnet, Remond, Bibb: black heroes all.

"True Bands":
Delaney and Whitfield-Holly—
all my troops though they stay home.
Gen'l Tubman took sick,
visions of an iron weight broken:

We wrote our names on the hideout walls
hung by the heavens in blood:

Mountains and swamps are belts
to the Great Black Way,
Shenandoah to Loudoun Heights:
forays to the mountaintop.
Arms and ammunition lost advance-guard:
success was fifty men like Shields Green.

We gained entry with crowbar.
The eastbound B&O train arrived,
and was let go, carrying panic
to Virginia, Maryland, Washington:
passenger-strewn scraps of insurrection
sifted from the fleeing train;
it took eleven hours for our munitions
to move three miles;
Lee arrived with marines;
we did not bargain our hostages.
I arrived with ague,
fever, a secret
on a long string broken,
standing on a powder magazine.

↗ ↗ ↗

PART TWO

↘↘↘↘↘↘↘↘

HEARTBLOW

"WHEN A WOMAN TAKE THE BLUES,
SHE TUCK HER HEAD AND CRY.
BUT WHEN A MAN CATCH THE BLUES,
HE GRAB HIS SHOES AND SLIDE."

NIGHTMARE BEGINS RESPONSIBILITY

RAT FEVER: HISTORY AS HALLUCINATION

A man's a man
when he can kill
rats with bare hands,
eat them
or be eaten by them.

Tracked leavings
on the village roof,
out the window
sewers overflowing;
a man's a man
when he can eat himself up
and leave no tracks.

↗↗↗

NEAR THE WHITE HOUSE

Across is a machine
in a ship's hull,
an anchor on the Potomac
is a mansion.
This black statue curtseys
in a vanilla smile,
its lips a cross
burning, its heat
flicking the mansion lights:
beacons on the marbleheads
and a sorrow song is a cross.

↗ ↗ ↗

THE MEANING OF PROTEST

Between the world and me
a black boy is a native
son with a long dream
if a white man will listen.
Uncle Tom's children
were eight men, all outsiders,
fish bellies living
underground.

Pagan Spain taught us the church
was woman as mystery, a penis
the sword to butcher each other;
Black Power! we're not going
to the moon, and in Bandung
white man can't come,
he's on a savage holiday.

Blossoms in a peanut field
won't bring me home;
something in the hum
of cotton is a glue
that won't hold red soil still;
ten million voices spliced
on an iron cross
between the world, and me, and you.

↗ ↗ ↗

TREE FEVER

Skin of trees cut down;
men in trees,
sacks of scrotum
breastmeat on brims,
soldier hats
on each father patroller,
posse the flag on picnic
their stars and stripes
our skin of scars.

↗ ↗ ↗

BIGGER'S BLUES

In this case
Mary's mama is correspondent:
blind witch with threaded
needles on the family table.
Ping-pong money to the poor.
Poor Mary gone off C.O.D.
in a golden trunk
head handed to her.
At the furnace where Bigger
hatted up, mama's
touching led him crazy
(what begins with N
and rhymes with Bigger)
on, on, on.

↗ ↗ ↗

PARABLE

Black-stemmed ax
stuck in white tree;
roots in waterhole
roped underground
get tree fever;
cut off handle,
tree die.

↗ ↗ ↗

HISTORY AS DIABOLICAL MATERNALISM

When I grind glass
I think of lenses
swallowed like sugar,
a preacher with glass eye,
a eunuch named Jesus,
Black Mary in his cottonfield.

↗ ↗ ↗

HEARTBLOW: MESSAGES

I sit in cubbyhole,
wasp nests north and south,
woods to the west, ocean east,
the highway north a southern road.
Goggle-eyed lamplights
blink uneven wattage
as the pulses
of your soulful heart.

I met a man who gave you bread
and meat and a warm bed
while you wrote *Black Boy*,
another who shared your Chicago loft;
some wait for released papers,
some salve old photographs.

A campus librarian near
Hollywood reads the unread
books to move with Bigger,
sees Mary's spittle as sperm
pushing her trunk,
holds the body as you hack her neck,
watches Bessie's downdraft
as a cross-corner shot.

That parable of black man, white woman,
the man's penis slung to his shin,
erect, foaming in that woman's womb,
the ambivalent female with smirk-shriek,
daylights of coitus stuck together,
through the nights the razored solution;
that the black man is nature,
the woman, on her drilled pedestal, divine,
the man with razor an artisan
in symmetry steel and sharp blades—
let him melt into his vat of precious metal,
let the female wipe her face of sperm,
let the black man's penis shrink to normal
service, let the posse eat their whips instead.

On the Seine I thought of you
on the towpath to Notre Dame;
at the Blue Note looking for Bud
on his *parisian thorofare;*
caught your blues from black musicians
while you died alone in prose;
some said you'd died of disconnection;
souls said you dealt your own heartblow.

↗ ↗ ↗

SPIRITUAL

Grandma's picket fence
balloon mask dancing
bloody moon your black ribcage.

↗↗↗

AFTERWORD: A FILM

Erect in the movies
with a new job,
Trader Horn
and *The Gay Woman*
unfold in a twinbill:
drums, wild dancing,
naked men, the silver
veils on the South Side.
He imagines nothing:
it is all before him,
born in a dream:
a gorilla broke loose
from his zoo
in a tuxedo: baboon.
You pick your red bottom.
The Daltons are the movies.

On my wall are pictures:
Jack Johnson, Joe Louis,
Harlow and Rogers:
"see the white god and die."

Underground I live in veils,
brick and cement,
the confession beaten out,
slung with hung carcasses,
a bloody cleaver grunting,
a dead baby in the sewer:
"all the people I saw were guilty."

Marked black I was shot,
double-conscious brother in the veil—
without an image of act or thought
double-conscious brother in the veil—

The rape: "Mrs. Dalton, it's me,
Bigger, I've brought Miss Dalton
home and she's drunk:"
to be the idea in these minds,
double-conscious brother in the veil—
father and leader where is my king,
veils of kingship will lead these folks
double-conscious brother in the veil—
"see the white gods and die"
double-conscious brother in the veil—

↗ ↗ ↗

PART THREE

↘↘↘↘↘↘↘↘

DEBRIDEMENT

DEBRIDEMENT

BLACK MEN ARE OAKS CUT DOWN.

CONGRESSIONAL MEDAL OF HONOR SOCIETY UNITED STATES OF AMERICA CHARTERED BY CONGRESS, AUGUST 14, 1958; THIS CERTIFIES THAT STAC JOHN HENRY LOUIS *IS A MEMBER OF THIS SOCIETY.*

"DON'T ASK ME ANYTHING ABOUT THE MEDAL. I DON'T EVEN KNOW HOW I WON IT."

DEBRIDEMENT: THE CUTTING AWAY OF DEAD OR CONTAMINATED TISSUE FROM A WOUND TO PREVENT INFECTION.

AMERICA: LOVE IT OR GIVE IT BACK.

CORKTOWN

Groceries ring
in my intestines:
grits aint groceries
eggs aint poultry
Mona Lisa was a man:
waltzing in sawdust
I dream my card
has five holes in it,
up to twenty holes;
five shots out of seven
beneath the counter;
surrounded by detectives
pale ribbons of valor
my necklace of bullets
powdering the operating table.

Five impaled men loop their ribbons
'round my neck
listening to whispers of valor:
"Honey, what you cryin' 'bout?
You made it back."

↗ ↗ ↗

SUBJECT REMEMBERS COMING
FACE TO FACE WITH VC WITH GUN;
REMEMBERS VC SQUEEZING TRIGGER;
GUN JAMMED. SUBJECT ENGAGED IN
MAGICAL THINKING RE: EPISODE:
GUILT-SURVIVOR; VALOR-MEDAL AWARD;
ONCE IN LIFETIME LOST COMPLETE CONTROL.
"WHAT WOULD HAPPEN IF I LOST CONTROL
IN DETROIT 'STEAD OF NAM?"

SUBJECT DEEPLY DISTURBED BY POSSIBILITY:

↗ ↗ ↗

CAVES

Four M-48 tank platoons ambushed
near Dak To, two destroyed:
the Ho Chi Minh Trail boils,
half my platoon rockets
into stars near Cambodia,
foot soldiers dance from highland woods
taxing our burning half:

there were no caves for them to hide.

We saw no action,
eleven months twenty-two days
in our old tank
burning sixty feet away:
I watch them burn inside out:
hoisting through heavy crossfire,
hoisting over turret hatches,
hoisting my last burning man
alive to the ground,
our tank artillery shells explode
killing all inside:
hoisting blown burned squad
in tank's bladder,
plug leaks with cave blood:

there were no caves for them to hide—

↗ ↗ ↗

SUBJECT HAS BAD DREAMS
SINCE RETURN FROM NAM;
WILL NOT CONFIDE IN WIFE/MOTHER;
ENTERTAINS MORAL JUDGMENTS RE: DAK TO:
WHY ORDERED TO SWITCH
TANKS NIGHT BEFORE? WHY HE
SPARED, NOT OTHERS?
GUILT-SURVIVOR! WAS HE SANE?
SUBJECT SAD, DEPRESSED:

↗ ↗ ↗

SITTING AT THE DAIS

I want to testify:

$10-plate-special-guest
at Cobo Hall, by Ford Motor,
by Chamber of Commerce,
General Westlessland at right arm:
*I was getting calls for him all
over Michigan: clamor didn't last:*
Lions, Rotary, American Legion,
Tiger Stadium—sit at the dais.

Ghetto mentality:
no tab
to credit card
to mortgage
to bad check made good by
                    black businessman
to college
to law school
to member of firm:
we'll pick up tab:

↗ ↗ ↗

SUBJECT PARALYZED BY THRUST UPON ALIEN CULTURE:

↗ ↗ ↗

I want to testify:

electronic nigger salute—
electronic-dais-poisoned-nigger-salute—

↗ ↗ ↗

SUBJECT UNABLE TO FORM PLAN
IN ALIEN CULTURE;
TRANSPORTED BY HAPPENSTANCE
ON OTHER SIDE OF GLOBE:
DISLOCATION—DISQUIETUDE:

↗ ↗ ↗

Seventy-five grand
and a good impression is a job:
fancy-brother-guest-of-honor-
dressed-in-blue:
I don't blow when on tour:
I don't shake hands when on tour:
I don't salute when on tour:
I don't suck salad fork when on tour:
I don't suck to presidents when on tour:

↗ ↗ ↗

*SUBJECT COMPLAINS OF SEVERE STOMACH
PAIN;*
MISSES WORK, APPOINTMENTS, TOURS;
REPORTS TO SELFRIDGE AIR FORCE BASE;
REPORTS TO VALLEY FORGE ARMY HOSPITAL;
$4999 DETROIT CREDIT UNION:
$1500 BACK PAY CASHIER'S CHECK, WALLET;
*SUBJECT TAKEN TO FREEDOMS FOUNDATION
TO SHAKE HANDS:*

*SUBJECT SAYS HE'LL GO AWOL IF MADE TO
GO AGAIN:*

↗ ↗ ↗

IN THE PROJECTS

Slung basketballs at Jeffries
House with some welfare kids
weaving in their figure eight hunger.

Mama asked if I was taking anything?
I rolled up my sleeves:
no tracks, mama:
"black-medal-man ain't street-poisoned,"
militants called:
"he's an electronic nigger!"

"Better keep electronic nigger 'way."
Electronic Nigger?
Mama, unplug me, please.

↗↗↗

SUBJECT DOUBTFUL OVER RE-ENTRY
AS RECRUITER; ARMY DIDN'T HONOR COM-
MITMENT:
"IF YOU EVER THINK ABOUT GETTING OUT,
LOOK ME UP"; WHEN CONTACTED THEY
DIDN'T REMEMBER:

"IT ALWAYS TOOK SEVERAL MINUTES TO RE-
MIND
THEM WHO I WAS." SUBJECT SIGNED OUT ON
3-DAY
PASS TO PHILADELPHIA: SUBJECT NEVER RE-
TURNED
AFTER CALLEY CONVICTION:

MURDERING VIETNAMESE CIVILIANS:

↗ ↗ ↗

DON'T LIST

When the Army calls
change your number:
while your bills lay unpaid
moisten mortgage foreclosure:
since credit union loan payment due,
deposit $25 wife's infected cyst:
because there are no more jobs for blacks
peddle my story: goes like this:
Sgt. STAC JOHN HENRY LOUIS is dead:
his home has been wiped clean:
no reason to change number.

↗ ↗ ↗

*FORD PICKS UP TWO YEAR LOANED THUN-
DERBIRD:*

SUBJECT PAYS $850 FOR MERCURY '67.

↗ ↗ ↗

A WHITE FRIEND FLIES
IN FROM THE COAST

Burned—black by birth,
burned—armed with .45,
burned—submachine gun,
burned—STAC hunted VC,
burned—killing 5–20,
burned—nobody know for sure;
burned—out of ammo,
burned—killed one with gun-stock,
burned—VC AK-47 jammed,

burned—killed faceless VC,
burned—over and over,
burned—STAC subdued by three men,
burned—three shots: morphine,
burned—tried killing prisoners,
burned—taken to Pleiku,
burned—held down, straitjacket,
burned—whites owe him, hear?
burned—I owe him, here.

↗ ↗ ↗

SUBJECT BRIGHT:
ARMY G. T. RATING=HIGH I. Q.;
DOES NOT VOLUNTEER INFORMATION;
NEVER KNEW DETROIT FATHER;
DID WHAT WAS EXPECTED OF HIM;
LOST TEMPER WHEN BULLY
PICKED ON YOUNGER BROTHER;
NEIGHBORS HAD TO DRAG HIM OFF.
SUBJECT LEARNED TO LIVE UP
TO EXPECTATION OF OTHERS:

ANGER-BUILD-UP-CONTINUALLY-SUPPRESSED:

SUBJECT BRIGHT:

↗ ↗ ↗

MAMA'S REPORT

Don't fight, honey,
don't let 'em catch you."

Tour over, gear packed,
hospital over, no job.

"Aw man, nothin' happened,"
explorer, altar boy—

Maybe it's 'cause they killed people
and don't know why they did?

My boy had color slides of dead people,
stacks of dead Vietnamese.

MP's asked if he'd been arrested
since discharge, what he'd been doin':

"Lookin' at slides,
lookin' at stacks of slides, mostly."

Fifteen minutes later a colonel called
from the Defense Department, said he'd won
                    the medal;

could he be in Washington with his family,
maybe he'd get a job now; he qualified.

The Democrats had lost, the president said;
there were signs of movement in Paris:

↗ ↗ ↗

MAALOX BLAND DIET PRESCRIBED;
GI SERIES CONDUCTED, NEGATIVE;
30-DAY CONVALESCENT LEAVE;
AWOL 90 DAYS; SUBJECT RETURN ARMY HOS-
PITAL;
BACKPAY, AWOL CHARGE DISMISSED;

SUBJECT AGREED TO PSYCHIATRIC EXAM;
DIVISION CHIEF PSYCHIATRIST ASSIGNED
DUE TO SUBJECT'S OUTSTANDING RECORD.

DIAGNOSIS: "POST-VIETNAM ADJUSTMENT DE-
PRESSION PROBLEM."

↗↗↗

CIRCLE OF BLOODS

All Detroit wanted some of him;
only-living-medal-of-honor-winner-
                    in-Michigan;
best-Detroit-recruiting-officer-factor-
since-blacks-biggest-manpower-pool:
all the lions circling
'round his Corktown fire.

↗ ↗ ↗

SUBJECT MARRIED, SPECIAL GUEST SUITE;
GUEST, NIXON INAUGURAL;
PERSONAL APPEARANCE SERIES ACROSS MICH-
IGAN
MAPPED BY ARMY.

↗ ↗ ↗

FIXING CERTIFICATES: DOG TAGS: LETTERS HOME

Our heliteam had mid-air blowout
dropping flares—5 burned alive.

The children carry hand
grenades to and from piss tubes.

Staring at tracer bullets
rice is the focal point of war.

On amphibious raid, our heliteam
found dead vc with maps of our compound.

On morning sick call you unzip;
before you piss you get a smear.

"VC reamed that *mustang* a new asshole"—
even at movies: "no round-eye pussy
                 no more"—

Tympanic membrane damage: high gone—
20–40 db loss mid-frequencies.

Scrub-typhus, malaria, dengue fever, cholera;
rotting buffalo, maggoted dog, decapped
children.

Bangkok: amber dust, watches, C-rations,
elephanthide billfolds, cameras, smack.

Sand&tinroof bunkers, 81/120 mm:
"Health record terminated this date by reason
of death."

Vacuolated amoeba, bacillary dysentery,
hookworm;
thorazine, tetracycline, darvon for diarrhea.

'Conitus': I wanna go home to mama;
Brown's mixture, ETH with codeine,
cortisone skin-creams.

Written on helipad fantail 600 bed *Repose;*
"no purple heart, hit by 'nother marine."

"Vascular repair, dissection, debridement":
sharp bone edges, mushy muscle, shrapnel:
                    stainless bucket.

Bodies in polyethylene bag: transport:
'Tan San Nhat Mortuary'

Blood, endotracheal tube, prep
abdomen, mid-chest to scrotum—

"While you're fixin' me doc,
can you fix them ingrown hairs on my face?"

"They didn't get my balls, did they?"
50 mg thorazine—"Yes they did, marine!"

↗ ↗ ↗

BLACK MEDICINE

Black medics=black eunuchs:
White lights=urge kill:
Black magic=cut tissue:
White vision=black remains:

↗ ↗ ↗

STREET-POISONED

Swans loom on the playground
swooning in the basket air,
the nod of their bills
in open flight, open formation.
Street-poisoned, a gray mallard
skims into our courtyard with a bag:

And he poisons them—
And he poisons them—

Electronic-nigger-recruiter,
my pass is a blade
near the sternum
cutting in:
you can make this a career.

Patches itch on my chest and shoulders—
I powder them with phisohex
solution from an aerosol can:
you can make this a career.

Pickets of insulin dab the cloudy
hallways in a spray.
Circuits of change
march to an honor guard—
I am prancing:
I am prancing:

you can make this a career.

↗ ↗ ↗

MAKIN' JUMP SHOTS

He waltzes into the lane
'cross the free-throw line,
fakes a drive, pivots,
floats from the asphalt turf
in an arc of black light,
and sinks two into the chains.

One on one he fakes
down the main, passes
into the free lane
and hits the chains.

A sniff in the fallen air—
he stuffs it through the chains
riding high:
"traveling" someone calls—
and he laughs, stepping
to a silent beat, gliding
as he sinks two into the chains.

↗ ↗ ↗

THIS IS CLINICAL HISTORY:

BODY POETRY TORN ASUNDER:

↗ ↗ ↗

WALKIN' UP NORTH IN MICHIGAN

I

I walk over deer dung,
looking at shrubs,
pheasant, frogs,
pacing deer herds,
grouse, ducks:
overshot,
deer browse declining
the melting snow grouse declining
aspen bud food declining
marsh, slough, wetland declining.

II

Clots of 2, 4-D,
2, 4, 5-T sift overhead:
mangroves splay and stick up;
hardwood forests shape
canopies in bamboo,
grass underbrush;
teak, rosewood, ebony,
camphor swim in cacodylic
acid to become rice
eaten by elephant, tiger,
monkey, pheasant, buffalo:
children declining
remember rice eaten.

↗↗↗

DEBRIDEMENT: OPERATION HARVEST MOON: *On Repose*

Stab incision below nipple,
left side; insert large chest tube;
sew to skin, right side;
catch blood from tube
in gallon drain bottle.
Wash abdomen with phisohex;
shave; spray brown iodine prep.

Stab incision below sternum
to symphis pubis;
catch blood left side;
sever reddish brown spleen
cut in half; tie off blood supply;
check retroperitoneal,
kidney, renal artery bleeding.

Dissect lateral wall
abdominal cavity; locate kidney;
pack colon, small intestine;
cut kidney; suture closely;
inch by inch check bladder,
liver, abdominal wall, stomach:
25 units blood, pressure down.

Venous pressure: 8; lumbar
musculature, lower spinal column
pulverized; ligate blood vessels,
right forearm; trim meat, bone ends;
tourniquet above fracture, left arm;
urine, negative: 4 hours; pressure
unstable; remove shrapnel flecks.

Roll on stomach; 35 units blood;
pressure zero; insert plastic blood
containers, pressure cuffs; pump chest
drainage tube; wash wounds sterile
saline; dress six-inch ace wraps;
wrap both legs, toe to groin; left arm
plaster, finger to shoulder: 40 units blood.

Pressure, pulse, respiration up;
remove bloody gowns; scrub; redrape;
5 cc vitamin K; thorazine: sixth
laparatomy; check hyperventilation;
stab right side incision below nipple;
insert large chest tube; catch blood
                    drain bottle . . .

↗ ↗ ↗

WAR NOTES: Stac to Son

GO directly to solarium
Do not pass *GO*
Do not collect $200

GROW pedicles
cover debridement
GO directly to solarium

Do not pass *GO*
GO directly to solarium
Do not collect $200

Cover debridement
Do not pass *GO*
GROW pedicles

↗ ↗ ↗

THE FAMILY OF DEBRIDEMENT

THEORY: INCONVENIENCED SUBJECT WILL
RETURN TO HOSPITAL IF LOANED
THUNDERBIRD
WITHDRAWN. HOPE: SUBJECT RETURNS,
TREATMENT:
FORECLOSURE FOR NINE MONTHS UNPAID
MORTGAGE;
WIFE TELLS SUBJECT HOSPITAL WANTS DE-
POSIT,
DISEASED CYST REMOVAL:
'AIN'T YOU GONNA GIVE ME A LITTLE KISS
GOOD-BYE'
SUBJECT-WIFE: TO RETURN WITH ROBE AND
CURLERS-
SUBJECT TELLS FRIEND HE'LL PAY $15 TO F'S
STEPFATHER IF HE'LL DRIVE HIM TO PICK UP
MONEY OWED HIM.

"THIS GUY LIVES DOWN THE STREET,
I DON'T WANT HIM TO SEE ME COMING."

*"IT LOOKED ODD FOR A CAR FILLED WITH
BLACKS
TO BE PARKED IN THE DARK IN A WHITE
NEIGHBORHOOD,
SO WE PULLED THE CAR OUT UNDER A
STREETLIGHT
SO EVERYBODY COULD SEE US."*

*STORE MANAGER: "I FIRST HIT HIM WITH
TWO BULLETS
SO I PULLED THE TRIGGER UNTIL MY GUN
WAS EMPTY."*

*"I'M GOING TO KILL YOU, YOU WHITE MF,"
STORE MANAGER
TOLD POLICE. POLICE TOOK CARLOAD, F AND
F'S PARENTS FOR
FURTHER QUESTIONING. SUBJECT DIED ON
OPERATING TABLE: 5 HRS:*

*SUBJECT BURIED ON GRASS SLOPE, 200 YARDS
EAST OF KENNEDY MEMORIAL,
OVERLOOKING POTOMAC AND PENTAGON,
TO THE SOUTH,
ARLINGTON NATIONAL CEMETERY.*

*ARMY HONOR GUARD
IN DRESS BLUES,
CARRIED OUT ASSIGNMENT
WITH PRECISION:*

↗ ↗ ↗